INSTRUCTIONS FOR USING SELF-COUNSEL'S LEGAL AND BUSINESS FORMS ON CD-ROM

DISCLAIMER

> The author, the publisher, and the vendor of these forms make no representations or warranties regarding the outcome or the use to which these forms are put and are not assuming any liability for any claims, losses, or damages arising out of the use of these forms. The user of these forms should not rely on the author or publisher of these forms for any professional advice.

Self-Counsel's Legal and Business Forms Kits on CD-ROM contain the following files with different extensions for your use, depending on what software you have on your computer:

1. If you use Microsoft Word 6.0 or higher, use the file with the extension ***.doc**

2. If you use Acrobat, use the file with the extension ***.pdf**

Follow these steps for using the .doc forms:

1. Using your word-processing software, open the appropriate file.

2. Complete the form according to your wishes. If instructions were included with the package, please be sure to read them as you go along. Note that the computer form has been designed to look as close as possible to the original Self-Counsel Press printed form provided. The final appearance of your computer form will depend upon what type of printer and word-processing software you are using. As a result, some modifications may be necessary. In particular, page breaks or blank lines may have to be inserted to ensure that related lines of text remain on the same page. You may wish to use the original Self-Counsel Press printed form as a rough guide. The computer form's design allows you to fill in all, some, or none of the blank sections before printing. Most of these blank sections are represented by a number of underscore characters like this "_____." Sometimes these sections may be too long for your computer to fit on the current line, resulting in text which may look like:

   name of person _____
   _____

   instead of:

   name of person _____

   If you do not wish to fill in the person's name just yet, then simply delete a few of the underscore characters until the blank section fits on the appropriate line.

3. Review your work.

4. Print and sign!

WILL FORM INSTRUCTIONS

Please be aware that there are statutory and common-law rules that govern the making and validity of wills, some of which may be unique to the province in which you reside. These may include laws that require certain people to be included among your beneficiaries. Accordingly, and due to the uniqueness of individual circumstances, it may be advisable to seek professional advice when drafting your will and, in any event, you should consult *Write Your Legal Will in 3 Easy Steps*, available from the Self-Counsel Press.

You should get legal advice if you —

(a) have a large or complex estate;

(b) are separated or contemplating divorce;

(c) are older and potentially subject to undue influence from possible beneficiaries;

(d) are contemplating marriage; or

(e) have questions about the will, any terms used in the form, or the type of gift you wish to make.

To complete your will, follow these steps:

(a) In the opening clause, fill in your complete legal name, address, and the date of writing the will.

(b) In *Clause 2*, insert the name and address of your executor (if male) or executrix (if female), as well as the name and address of an alternative executor or executrix. These people are the persons who will carry out your instructions and must be of legal age.

(c) In *Clause 4*, specify the number of days (usually 30) that a beneficiary must live to be deemed to have survived you. Specify the bequests (i.e., the gifts) that you wish to give, including the names and addresses of the persons ("beneficiaries") to whom such bequests are to be given. Always provide for the "residue" of your estate (i.e., anything other than what is specifically mentioned).

(d) Sign the will in the presence of two adult witnesses. (If you are male, you are the testator; if female, the testatrix.)

(e) Have two witnesses sign in the presence of each other and yourself. They should include their addresses and occupations. **Note: The witnesses to the will must not be individuals to whom gifts are made, or closely related to anyone to whom gifts are made.**

LIVING WILL AND ADVANCE MEDICAL DIRECTIVE INSTRUCTIONS

Remember that a living will or an advance medical directive is an expression of your wishes only; it has no legal validity. You have no guarantee that it will be binding upon your physician, relatives, or the hospital in which you are being cared for.

Don't put these documents with your will, which is looked at only after your death. Put them in a place where your relatives can find them and tell them where it is, or, better yet, give them copies. To make the best use of your living will and advance medical directive, follow these steps.

(a) Sign and date them before two witnesses. (This helps ensure that you signed of your own free will and not under any pressure.)

(b) Discuss the requests with your doctor to make sure that he or she is in agreement. Leave copies with your doctor for your medical file.

(c) Give copies to those most likely to be concerned if the time comes when you no longer take part in the decisions for your own future. Enter their names on the bottom line of the living will and advance medical directive. Keep the original nearby, easily and readily available.

(d) Above all, discuss your intentions with those closest to you, *now*.

(e) It is a good idea to look over your living will and advance medical directive once a year and redate them and initial the new date to make it clear that your wishes are unchanged.

(f) Ask a lawyer to incorporate the last paragraph of the living will in your actual will.

For more information, you may want to refer to *Write Your Legal Will in 3 Easy Steps,* published by Self-Counsel Press.

ESTATE AND BUSINESS PLANNING GUIDE INSTRUCTIONS

The Estate and Business Planning Guide does not take the place of a will. It is meant for setting up a practical plan for the management and distribution of your assets after your death. Revise it periodically and keep it in an easy-to-find place.

ENDURING POWER OF ATTORNEY INSTRUCTIONS

Please be aware that each province has its own laws governing Power of Attorney. It may be advisable to discuss your concerns with a professional, as well as the person whom you would like to appoint as your attorney. For more information, consult Self-Counsel Press's *Write Your Legal Will in 3 Easy Steps* or your province's Power of Attorney Act.

This is the
Last Will and Testament

of me,_____, of the

_____ of_____ in the Province of
(City, Municipality, Town, District)

_____, made the_____ day of_____.
(Date)

    1.   I REVOKE all former Wills, Codicils, and Testamentary Dispositions previously made by me.

    2.   I APPOINT_____ of the

_____ of_____ in the Province of
(City, Municipality, Town, District)

_____, to be the Execut_____ of this my last Will and Testament.
(or/rix)

BUT IF my said Execut_____ should refuse to act, predecease me, or die within a period
(or/rix)

of_____ days following my death, THEN I APPOINT_____

_____ of the_____ of_____
(City, Municipality, Town, District)

in the Province of_____ to be the Execut_____ of this my last Will
(or/rix)

and Testament.

    3.   I DIRECT all my just debts, funeral and testamentary expenses, all succession duties,inheritance and death taxes, and all expenses necessarily incidental thereto, to be paid and satisfied by my Execut_____ as soon as conveniently may be after my death.
(or/rix)

4. Any beneficiary who dies within a period of_____ days following my death will be deemed not to have survived me, and their gift will then become part of the residue of my estate.

    a) I DISTRIBUTE my assets as follows:

    b) I DISTRIBUTE any residue of my estate as follows:

5. I give my Execut_____ the following POWERS:
      (or/rix)

6. I APPOINT _____

of the_____ of_____ in the province of
    (City, Municipality, Town, District)

_____ as Guardian(s) of my minor children, BUT IF_____

_____ should refuse to act, predecease me, or die within a

period of_____days following my death, THEN I APPOINT_____

of the_____ of_____ in the province of
    (City, Municipality, Town, District)

_____ as Guardian(s) of my minor children.

I request that my Guardians:

IN WITNESS whereof I have set my hand the day and year first above written.

_____
(Signature)

This page was signed and the preceding pages were initialled
by the Testat_____ and published and declared as and for
         (or/rix)

_____ last Will and Testament in the presence of us both
(his/her)
present together at the same time who at_____
                                   (his/her)
request and in_____ presence and in the presence of
              (his/her)
each other have hereunto subscribed our names as witnesses:

Name_____
                    (Signature)

Address_____

Occupation_____

Name_____
                    (Signature)

Address_____

Occupation_____

SELF-COUNSEL PRESS—CDN-W (2-3)01

DATED _____ 20___

Will

—OF—

| | | | |

This is the
Last Will and Testament

of me,_____, of the

_____ of_____ in the Province of
(City, Municipality, Town, District)

_____, made the_____ day of_____.
(Date)

1. I REVOKE all former Wills, Codicils, and Testamentary Dispositions previously made by me.

2. I APPOINT_____ of the

_____ of_____ in the Province of
(City, Municipality, Town, District)

_____, to be the Execut_____ of this my last Will and Testament.
(or/rix)

BUT IF my said Execut_____ should refuse to act, predecease me, or die within a period
(or/rix)

of_____ days following my death, THEN I APPOINT_____

_____ of the_____ of_____
(City, Municipality, Town, District)

in the Province of_____ to be the Execut_____ of this my last Will
(or/rix)

and Testament.

3. I DIRECT all my just debts, funeral and testamentary expenses, all succession duties,inheritance and death taxes, and all expenses necessarily incidental thereto, to be paid and satisfied by my Execut____ as soon as conveniently may be after my death.
(or/rix)

4. Any beneficiary who dies within a period of_____ days following my death will be deemed not to have survived me, and their gift will then become part of the residue of my estate.

a) I DISTRIBUTE my assets as follows:

b) I DISTRIBUTE any residue of my estate as follows:

5. I give my Execut_____ the following POWERS:
        (or/rix)

6. I APPOINT _____

of the_____ of_____ in the province of
        (City, Municipality, Town, District)

_____ as Guardian(s) of my minor children, BUT IF_____

_____ should refuse to act, predecease me, or die within a

period of_____days following my death, THEN I APPOINT_____

of the_____ of_____ in the province of
        (City, Municipality, Town, District)

_____ as Guardian(s) of my minor children.

I request that my Guardians:

IN WITNESS whereof I have set my hand the day and year first above written.

_____
(Signature)

This page was signed and the preceding pages were initialled

by the Testat_____ and published and declared as and for
      (or/rix)

_____ last Will and Testament in the presence of us both
(his/her)

present together at the same time who at_____
                             (his/her)

request and in_____ presence and in the presence of
      (his/her)

each other have hereunto subscribed our names as witnesses:

Name_____
                    (Signature)

Address_____

Occupation_____

Name_____
                    (Signature)

Address_____

Occupation_____

DATED _____ 20 ___

Will

—OF—

_____

_____

_____

_____

ADVANCE MEDICAL DIRECTIVE

This is the Living Will and Medical Directive of_____,
currently resident at_____.

1. Effective:

a. I recognize that a time may come when by reason of illness or mental incapacity I cannot participate in my medical care or health decisions. This directive will be in effect only while I am unable to make or communicate my own decisions by speaking, by writing, or by gesturing.

2. My Agent:

a. I appoint as my Agent to make personal and health and medical care decisions on my behalf when I no longer have the capacity to make such decisions_____ _____, currently resident at_____.

b. If_____ is unwilling or unable to act as my Agent, then I appoint the first person on the following list who is able and willing to serve as my Alternate Agent:

_____ of_____
_____ of_____
_____ of_____

c. If my spouse has been designated as an Agent or Alternate Agent above, and if after the execution of this document, my spouse and I are legally separated or divorced, any rights and powers granted to my spouse by this document shall immediately terminate on such legal separation or divorce.

d. Any reference to Agent in this document shall include the meaning Alternate Agent where such Alternate Agent is acting as provided in this document.

3. Power of Agent:

a. I grant to my Agent the full power and authority to make all decisions affecting my health care and living arrangements and I request that my Agent follow my Wishes as indicated in this document. If I have not included instructions on any particular matter that may arise, I hereby empower my Agent to act as he or she thinks best, but in accordance with his or her comprehension of my wishes, values, and beliefs.

b. I grant to my Agent the full power and authority to:

- sign documents, including but not restricted to releases, permissions, or waivers;
- review and disclose medical records;
- hire or discharge caregivers;
- authorize admission to or release from medical facilities;
- consent, refuse, or withdraw consent to any form of health care.

4. Visiting Rights:

I hereby request that all medical or care facilities in which I may be placed give to my Agent primary visiting rights as well as the right to admit or exclude other visitors.

5. My Wishes:

a. If the situation should arise in which there is no reasonable expectation of my recovery from physical or mental disability, then I request that medication be mercifully administered to me to alleviate suffering and that I be allowed to die and not be kept alive by artificial means. I do not fear death itself as much as the indignities of deterioration, dependence, and hopeless pain. In particular, I have the following instructions:

_____

_____

_____

b. If it becomes necessary for a Guardian of my person to be appointed under the appropriate law of the province, then I nominate my Agent, as appointed under clause 2 of this document, as my choice for Guardian.

c. If any dispute arises about the interpretation of my Wishes or about the validity of this Directive, then I encourage my Agent to seek to avoid litigation and to pursue all reasonable ways to resolve the dispute, including mediation.

6. Additional matters:

a. I hereby revoke any previous living wills, personal directives, or advance medical directives.

b. I hereby indemnify and hold harmless my Agent and anyone who acts in good faith at the behest of my Agent in fulfilling my Wishes as expressed in this document.

7. Signature:

I,_____, of_____, being of sound mind, confirm that I understand the content of this document and the power that it gives to my Agent and further confirm that this document represents my Wishes.

DATED at_____,
on this_____ day of_____, 200___.

SIGNED_____ (_____)
in the presence of:

WITNESS_____ (_____)

WITNESS_____ (_____)

ADVANCE MEDICAL DIRECTIVE

This is the Living Will and Medical Directive of_____,

currently resident at_____.

1. Effective:

a. I recognize that a time may come when by reason of illness or mental incapacity I cannot participate in my medical care or health decisions. This directive will be in effect only while I am unable to make or communicate my own decisions by speaking, by writing, or by gesturing.

2. My Agent:

a. I appoint as my Agent to make personal and health and medical care decisions on my behalf when I no longer have the capacity to make such decisions_____

_____,

currently resident at_____.

b. If_____ is unwilling or unable to act as my Agent, then I appoint the first person on the following list who is able and willing to serve as my Alternate Agent:

_____ of _____
_____ of _____
_____ of _____

c. If my spouse has been designated as an Agent or Alternate Agent above, and if after the execution of this document, my spouse and I are legally separated or divorced, any rights and powers granted to my spouse by this document shall immediately terminate on such legal separation or divorce.

d. Any reference to Agent in this document shall include the meaning Alternate Agent where such Alternate Agent is acting as provided in this document.

3. Power of Agent:

a.   I grant to my Agent the full power and authority to make all decisions affecting my health care and living arrangements and I request that my Agent follow my Wishes as indicated in this document. If I have not included instructions on any particular matter that may arise, I hereby empower my Agent to act as he or she thinks best, but in accordance with his or her comprehension of my wishes, values, and beliefs.

b.   I grant to my Agent the full power and authority to:

- sign documents, including but not restricted to releases, permissions, or waivers;
- review and disclose medical records;
- hire or discharge caregivers;
- authorize admission to or release from medical facilities;
- consent, refuse, or withdraw consent to any form of health care.

4. Visiting Rights:

I hereby request that all medical or care facilities in which I may be placed give to my Agent primary visiting rights as well as the right to admit or exclude other visitors.

5. My Wishes:

a.   If the situation should arise in which there is no reasonable expectation of my recovery from physical or mental disability, then I request that medication be mercifully administered to me to alleviate suffering and that I be allowed to die and not be kept alive by artificial means. I do not fear death itself as much as the indignities of deterioration, dependence, and hopeless pain. In particular, I have the following instructions:

_____

_____

_____

b.   If it becomes necessary for a Guardian of my person to be appointed under the appropriate law of the province, then I nominate my Agent, as appointed under clause 2 of this document, as my choice for Guardian.

c.   If any dispute arises about the interpretation of my Wishes or about the validity of this Directive, then I encourage my Agent to seek to avoid litigation and to pursue all reasonable ways to resolve the dispute, including mediation.

6. Additional matters:

a.   I hereby revoke any previous living wills, personal directives, or advance medical directives.

b.   I hereby indemnify and hold harmless my Agent and anyone who acts in good faith at the behest of my Agent in fulfilling my Wishes as expressed in this document.

7. Signature:

I,_____, of_____, being of sound mind, confirm that I understand the content of this document and the power that it gives to my Agent and further confirm that this document represents my Wishes.

DATED at_____,
on this_____ day of_____, 200___.

SIGNED_____ (_____)
in the presence of:

WITNESS_____ (_____)

WITNESS_____ (_____)

Living Will

TO MY FAMILY, MY PHYSICIAN,
MY LAWYER, MY CLERIC

TO ANY MEDICAL FACILITY IN WHOSE CARE
I HAPPEN TO BE

TO ANY INDIVIDUAL WHO MAY BECOME RESPONSIBLE
FOR MY HEALTH, WELFARE, OR AFFAIRS

    Death is as much a reality as birth, growth, maturity, and old age. It is the one certainty of life. If the time comes when I,_____,

(your name in full)

can no longer take part in decisions for my own future, let this statement stand as an expression of my wishes, while I am still of sound mind.

If the situation should arise in which there is no reasonable expectation of my recovery from physical or mental disability, then I request that medication be mercifully administered to me to alleviate suffering, and that I be allowed to die and not be kept alive by artificial means. I do not fear death itself as much as the indignities of deterioration, dependence, and hopeless pain. In particular, I have the following instructions:_____

_____

_____

_____

_____

This request is made after careful consideration. I hope you who care for me will feel morally bound to follow its mandate. I recognize that this appears to place heavy responsibility on you, but it is with the intention of relieving you of such responsibility and of placing it on myself in accordance with my strong convictions, that this statement is made.

_____   _____
(Date)   *(Signature)*

_____   Copies of this request have been given to:
(Witness)

                                       _____

_____   _____
(Witness)

Living Will

TO MY FAMILY, MY PHYSICIAN,
MY LAWYER, MY CLERIC

TO ANY MEDICAL FACILITY IN WHOSE CARE
I HAPPEN TO BE

TO ANY INDIVIDUAL WHO MAY BECOME RESPONSIBLE
FOR MY HEALTH, WELFARE, OR AFFAIRS

    Death is as much a reality as birth, growth, maturity, and old age. It is the one certainty of life. If the time comes when I,_____,

(your name in full)

can no longer take part in decisions for my own future, let this statement stand as an expression of my wishes, while I am still of sound mind.

If the situation should arise in which there is no reasonable expectation of my recovery from physical or mental disability, then I request that medication be mercifully administered to me to alleviate suffering, and that I be allowed to die and not be kept alive by artificial means. I do not fear death itself as much as the indignities of deterioration, dependence, and hopeless pain. In particular, I have the following instructions:_____

_____

_____

_____

_____

This request is made after careful consideration. I hope you who care for me will feel morally bound to follow its mandate. I recognize that this appears to place heavy responsibility on you, but it is with the intention of relieving you of such responsibility and of placing it on myself in accordance with my strong convictions, that this statement is made.

_____	_____
(Date)	*(Signature)*
_____	Copies of this request have been given to:
(Witness)	
	_____
_____	_____
(Witness)	_____

SELF-COUNSEL PRESS—LIVWILL (4-1)01

ENDURING POWER OF ATTORNEY

I,_____ of the_____
                                                    (City, Municipality, Town, District)

of_____, in the Province/Territory of_____, state:

    1.   I REVOKE all former Enduring Powers of Attorney previously given by me.

    2.   I APPOINT_____ of the_____ of
                                                                  (City, Municipality, Town, District)

_____ in the Province/Territory of_____ to be my attorney.

BUT IF my said attorney should refuse to act, or predecease me, THEN I APPOINT
_____ of the_____
                                                    (City, Municipality, Town, District)

of_____ in the Province/Territory of_____
to be my attorney.

    3.   This power of attorney will be EFFECTIVE UPON_____,
subject to the written declaration of_____.

    4.   My attorney has the POWER TO carry out the following:

    5.   My attorney is RESTRICTED FROM the following:

6. My attorney shall RECEIVE PAYMENT on the following terms:

7. IF this Enduring Power of Attorney is the cause of any disagreement, my attorney may:

Dated at_____

This_____ day of_____ in 200___

Signed_____

Name of Witness (print)_____

Signature of Witness_____

ENDURING POWER OF ATTORNEY

I,_____ of the_____
(City, Municipality, Town, District)

of_____, in the Province/Territory of_____, state:

1. I REVOKE all former Enduring Powers of Attorney previously given by me.

2. I APPOINT_____ of the_____ of
(City, Municipality, Town, District)

_____ in the Province/Territory of_____ to be my attorney.

BUT IF my said attorney should refuse to act, or predecease me, THEN I APPOINT
_____ of the_____
(City, Municipality, Town, District)

of_____ in the Province/Territory of_____
to be my attorney.

3. This power of attorney will be EFFECTIVE UPON_____,
subject to the written declaration of_____.

4. My attorney has the POWER TO carry out the following:

5. My attorney is RESTRICTED FROM the following:

6.   My attorney shall RECEIVE PAYMENT on the following terms:

7.   IF this Enduring Power of Attorney is the cause of any disagreement, my attorney may:

Dated at_____

This_____ day of_____ in 200___

Signed_____

Name of Witness (print)_____

Signature of Witness_____

SELF-COUNSEL PRESS
ESTATE PLANNING & INVENTORY
REVISE PERIODICALLY AND KEEP IN AN EASY-TO-FIND PLACE
(THIS DOES NOT TAKE THE PLACE OF A WILL)

Mr. / Mrs.
Miss / Ms. _____ S.I.N.# _____

Of (residence) _____

Place of birth _____ Citizenship _____ Date of birth _____

Occupation _____

Business address _____

Business telephone number ( ) _____ Residence telephone number ( ) _____

Fax ( ) _____ E-mail _____

Employer_____ Employer's telephone number ( ) _____

Fax ( ) _____ E-mail _____

Marital Status: Single [ ]   Married [ ]   Widowed [ ]   Divorced [ ]   Separated [ ]

Date of marriage _____ Place of marriage _____

Have you made a Will? _____ Date executed _____

Where is it? _____

Spouse's name _____ Date of birth _____

Has spouse made a Will? _____ Date executed _____

Where is it? _____

Were you or your spouse ever married previously? _____

If so, name and address of previous spouse? _____

_____

Names of children	Date of birth	Married or single	Number and age of grandchildren

Are any of the children adopted or stepchildren of yourself? _____

If so, which ones? _____ Of your spouse? _____

_____ _____

	Date of birth	Occupation	Where is Will and who is Executor/trix
Parents: of yourself			
Parents: of spouse			

Professional advisers (give names and addresses)

_____

(Lawyer)   (Address)

_____

(Accountant)   (Address)

_____

(Insurance Agent)   (Address)

_____

(Bank)   (Address)

_____

(Trust Company)   (Address)

_____

(Doctor)   (Address)

_____

Others:

Location of important documents:

Birth certificate: _____   Life insurance policies: _____

Marriage certificate: _____   Safety deposit box: _____

Deeds: _____   Bank accounts: _____

Divorce judgment: _____   Financial records: _____

Tax returns: _____   Pension plans: _____

Stocks/bonds: _____   Notes/mortgages: _____

YOUR ESTATE PLAN REQUIREMENTS

a. TO PROVIDE FOR:

Name	Relationship	Date of birth

b. ESTATE FUNDS NEEDED FOR SPOUSE

FOR PERIODIC UPDATING

		Month Year	Month Year	Month Year
MONTHLY INCOME TO SPOUSE COMMENCING AT AGE	_____	_____	_____	_____
MONTHLY INCOME REQUIRED	_____	_____	_____	_____
DEDUCT AMOUNT PROVIDED BY CPP/QPP, OLD AGE SUPPLEMENT AND PROVINCIAL GOVERNMENT PROGRAMS	_____	_____	_____	_____
BALANCE REQUIRED (commuted value over lifetime — see attached Table I)	_____	_____	_____	_____

c. ESTATE FUNDS NEEDED FOR CHILDREN

MONTHLY INCOME TO CHILDREN UNTIL AGE	_____	_____	_____	_____
MONTHLY INCOME REQUIRED	_____	_____	_____	_____
DEDUCT AMOUNT PROVIDED BY CPP/QP	_____	_____	_____	_____
BALANCE REQUIRED	_____	_____	_____	_____
TOTAL NUMBER OF YEARS UNTIL YOUNGEST IS OF AGE	_____	_____	_____	_____
BALANCE REQUIRED (commuted value over lifetime — see attached Table II)	_____	_____	_____	_____

d. EDUCATIONAL FUND TO PROVIDE FOR:

	Month Year	Month Year	Month Year
_____	_____	_____	_____
_____	_____	_____	_____
_____	_____	_____	_____
_____	_____	_____	_____
_____	_____	_____	_____
_____	_____	_____	_____
_____	_____	_____	_____
_____	_____	_____	_____
TOTAL	_____		

e. ESTIMATED MISCELLANEOUS EXPENSES

	Month Year	Month Year	Month Year
MORTGAGE REDEMPTION FUND (if mortgage life insured)	_____	_____	_____
EMERGENCY FUND	_____	_____	_____
FUNERAL EXPENSES (approximately)	_____	_____	_____
DEBTS	_____	_____	_____
LAWYER, PROBATE, AND EXECUTOR FEES Allow for size of estate and complicated assets (6% of gross value)	_____	_____	_____
TOTAL	_____	_____	_____
f. TOTAL ESTATE REQUIRED	_____	_____	_____

YOUR ESTATE BALANCE SHEET

FOR PERIODIC UPDATING

a. LIQUID ASSETS

		Month Year	Month Year	Month Year
CASH-ON-HAND (average amount held in accounts)	_____	_____	_____	_____
		_____	_____	_____
		_____	_____	_____
BONDS (face amount)	_____	_____	_____	_____
		_____	_____	_____
		_____	_____	_____
STOCKS (market value)	_____	_____	_____	_____
		_____	_____	_____
		_____	_____	_____
LIFE INSURANCE Policies you own on your own life (face value)	_____	_____	_____	_____
Policies owned by you on lives of others (surrender value)	_____	_____	_____	_____
PENSION FUND — DEATH BENEFIT	_____	_____	_____	_____
GROUP INSURANCE AND SURVIVOR BENEFITS	_____	_____	_____	_____
REGISTERED RETIREMENT SAVINGS PLAN	_____	_____	_____	_____
ANNUITY CONTRACTS Notes and accounts receivable	_____	_____	_____	_____
		_____	_____	_____
Other (specify)	_____	_____	_____	_____
		_____	_____	_____
TOTAL LIQUID ASSETS	_____	_____	_____	_____

SELF-COUNSEL PRESS—CDN-ESTATE (5-5)01

b. NONLIQUID ASSETS

		Month Year	Month Year	Month Year

RESIDENCE — In whose name?
(market value less mortgages)

OTHER REAL ESTATE
(as above)

INTEREST IN PRIVATE BUSINESSES
(Note: If a buy-sell agreement is involved, list face value of insurance policy which your estate will receive in event of your death.)

MORTGAGES OR AGREEMENTS FOR SALE OWNED

				Month Year			Month Year		
1	2	3		1	2	3	1	2	3

Mortgagor/Borrower

Amortization period

Maturity date

Principal amount

Total current value
of mortgages (see Table III)

PROPERTY LIKELY TO COME TO YOU FROM GIFTS OR INHERITANCE IN NEAR FUTURE

PERSONAL EFFECTS
Motor vehicles

Furniture

Jewelry, furs, artwork, and other articles of special value

Hobby and recreational equipment

Other

_____	_____	_____	_____
_____	_____	_____	_____
_____	_____	_____	_____
_____	_____	_____	_____
_____	_____	_____	_____
_____	_____	_____	_____

TOTAL NONLIQUID ASSETS _____ | _____ | _____ | _____

ADD TOTAL OF ALL ASSETS _____ | _____ | _____ | _____

c. LIABILITIES
(mortgages and other real estate
encumbrances excluded —
see above)

PERSONAL DEBTS
(including personal bank loans,
finance company loans, alimony
payments, etc.)

LOANS ON LIFE INSURANCE
POLICIES

HOUSEHOLD ACCOUNTS
PAYABLE
(average monthly total)

MISCELLANEOUS

TOTAL

d. TOTALS

TOTAL ASSETS

MINUS TOTAL LIABILITIES

EQUALS*
(*This is the total available to meet
estate requirements)

MINUS TOTAL ESTATE REQUIRED

EQUALS
(Shortage or surplus)

TABLE I
FEMALE LIFE ANNUITY

(assumes 10 years' guarantee)
For males cost is approximately 9% less

AGE	*TO PROVIDE EACH $100 MONTHLY INCOME, YOU NEED
25	15 900
30	15 690
35	15 440
40	15 130
45	14 670
50	14 100
55	13 460
60	12 800

*For example, to provide a monthly income of $1000 per month to a female at age 60 you will need $128 000

TABLE II
ANNUITY CERTAIN

(All rates are approximate)

YEARS TO RUN	TO PROVIDE EACH $100 MONTHLY INCOME, YOU NEED
1	1 100
2	2 250
3	3 200
4	4 170
5	5 100
6	5 870
7	6 570
8	7 200
9	7 790
10	8 320
11	8 800
12	9 240
13	9 650
14	10 020
15	10 350
16	10 660
17	10 960
18	11 250
19	11 520
20	11 780

TABLE III
MORTGAGE BALANCE PER $1 000 INITIAL AMOUNT

20-year amortization

Start of year	10%	11%	12%	13%	14%	15%	16%	17%	18%
1	1 000	1 000	1 000	1 000	1 000	1 000	1000	1000	1 000
2	983	985	987	989	990	991	993	993	994
3	965	969	973	976	979	981	984	986	988
4	945	951	956	961	966	970	973	977	980
5	923	931	938	945	951	956	961	966	970
6	898	908	917	926	934	941	947	953	958
7	871	883	894	905	914	923	931	938	945
8	841	855	868	880	891	902	911	920	928
9	807	823	838	852	865	877	889	899	908
10	771	788	805	821	835	849	862	874	885
11	730	749	767	785	801	816	831	844	857
12	685	706	725	744	761	778	794	809	823
13	636	657	677	697	716	734	751	767	782
14	581	603	624	644	664	682	700	718	734
15	521	542	563	584	603	623	641	659	677
16	454	475	495	515	534	554	572	590	608
17	380	399	418	437	455	473	491	508	525
18	299	315	332	348	364	380	396	411	427
19	209	221	234	246	259	272	284	297	309
20	110	117	124	131	138	146	153	161	168

25-year amortization

Start of year	10%	11%	12%	13%	14%	15%	16%	17%	18%
1	1 000	1 000	1 000	1 000	1 000	1 000	1000	1000	1 000
2	991	992	993	994	995	996	997	997	998
3	980	983	986	988	990	991	993	994	995
4	969	973	977	981	984	986	988	990	992
5	956	962	967	972	976	980	983	986	988
6	942	950	957	963	968	973	977	980	983
7	926	936	944	952	959	964	969	974	978
8	909	920	930	940	948	955	961	966	971
9	890	903	915	926	935	943	951	957	963
10	869	884	897	910	921	930	939	947	954
11	846	862	878	891	904	915	925	934	942
12	820	838	855	871	885	898	909	919	929
13	792	812	830	847	863	877	890	902	912
14	760	782	802	820	838	853	868	881	893
15	726	749	770	790	809	826	842	856	870
16	688	712	734	755	775	794	811	827	842
17	645	670	694	716	737	757	775	793	809
18	599	624	648	671	693	714	733	752	769
19	547	572	597	620	642	664	684	704	722
20	491	515	539	562	584	606	626	646	665
21	428	451	473	496	517	538	559	579	598
22	358	379	400	420	441	460	479	498	517
23	282	299	317	225	352	369	387	403	420
24	197	210	224	237	251	264	278	291	304
25	103	111	119	126	134	142	150	158	166

CHECKLIST

When death occurs to a close friend or relative, time loses its meaning. Don't panic and don't rush. There is nothing more you can do for the deceased.

Use the following checklist to your best advantage.

Note: This checklist is not all-encompassing, so use it only as a guide.

1. When death occurs at home, contact the following:
    - (   ) Doctor and/or ambulance
    - (   ) Close family or personal friend for guidance and help
    - (   ) Religious advisor, if applicable
    - (   ) All those who must be told
    - (   ) Babysitter, dog kennel, etc. — all those who will take the load off you for a few days
    - (   ) If parts of the body are to be donated for medical or research purposes, contact institutions involved

2. When death occurs at hospital, you will be contacted by the doctor. You carry on from there.

3. If death occurs as a result of an accident, contact a lawyer (and police, if not already notified) as soon as possible.

4. Arrange disposition of the body. Determine how to dispose of the body. Deceased may have left specific instructions regarding this. If not, remember service is for the benefit of close friends and relatives, not the deceased, so arrange accordingly.
    - (   ) Contact memorial society or funeral home for arrangement of service.
    - (   ) Contact religious advisor regarding these arrangements.
    - (   ) Attend funeral or cremation.

5. Cancel deliveries, service calls, subscriptions, appointments, etc., on behalf of the deceased.

6. If you are a spouse or dependent person, make sure you have enough cash on hand to see you through the next few months. (For a complete explanation of which assets can be quickly turned into ready cash, see Self-Counsel Press's *Write Your Legal Will in 3 Easy Steps.*)

7. Obtain death certificate (usually from the doctor).

8. Arrange to publish death notice in local newspaper.

9. Find the will. Usually it will be in the safety deposit box or in some place where all such important papers are kept.

10. Find out from the will who is to be the executor (if unknown). If there is no will, an administrator will have to be appointed, usually the closest relative.

11. Contact lawyer and executor to begin probate of estate and disposition of assets.

12. The following organizations or departments may need to be contacted on behalf of the deceased:

(**Note:** Before completing any of the following tasks, check with the executor first as this may be something he or she is instructed to do in the deceased's will.)

(   ) **Bank(s):** Cancel or transfer account(s) of the deceased (joint accounts should be dealt with by the joint owner of the account).

(   ) **RRSPs, Stocks, and Bonds:** Notify the appropriate institutions regarding RRSPs, stocks, and bonds. These may have a named beneficiary and the institutions should contact the beneficiary named.

(   ) **Canadian Pension Plan Death/Survivor Benefits:** Contact the Canadian Pension Plan offices because the person taking financial responsibility for the funeral costs may be eligible for this benefit.

(   ) **Company Pension Plan:** Check the work records of the deceased for information regarding personal contribution to a work pension plan. Contact the human resources department of the deceased's workplace for more information.

(   ) **Employee Benefits:** Call the human resources department to find out if there was insurance coverage or death benefits.

(   ) **Insurance Policies:** Check the deceased's files for any insurance policies and contact the appropriate agencies on what to do next.

(   ) **Credit Card(s):** Contact the credit card company regarding any outstanding balances and for information on returning or destroying the deceased's credit cards.

(   ) **Income Tax:** File a final tax return by April 30 of the year following the death.

(   ) **Provincial Health Insurance:** Contact the health insurance office to find out what to do with the deceased's card and payment of any outstanding bills.

(   ) **Veterans' Benefits:** Contact the Department of Veterans' Affairs, if applicable.

(   ) **Worker's Compensation:** Contact the Worker's Compensation Board if the person's death was caused in a work-related accident.

(   ) **Passport, Driver's License, or Other Personal Identification:** Contact the appropriate agencies for instructions on what to do with the deceased's identification.

Have You Made Your Will?
Complete Kit
Serial #: SCPW-3352-GCUC-5779

My Will

ISBN 1-55180-591-X

VERSION 04 – 1

Windows Setup

1. Insert CD into CD-ROM drive
2. Follow onscreen instructions

©2004 Self-Counsel Press

• Forms

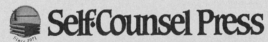

Self·Counsel Press

1481 Charlotte Road, North Vancouver, BC   V7J 1H1
Tel: (604) 986-3366 Fax: (604) 986-3947
Toll free: 1-800-663-3007

www.self-counsel.com